STALIN'S FEISTY GUEST

STALIN'S FEISTY GUEST

Marjorie Hope

Copyright © 2015 by Marjorie Hope.

Library of Congress Control Number: 2015903853
ISBN:
  Hardcover   978-1-5035-5157-2
  Softcover   978-1-5035-5158-9
  eBook   978-1-5035-5159-6

All rights reserved. No part of this book may be reproduced or transmitted in any form or by any means, electronic or mechanical, including photocopying, recording, or by any information storage and retrieval system, without permission in writing from the copyright owner.

Any people depicted in stock imagery provided by Thinkstock are models, and such images are being used for illustrative purposes only. Certain stock imagery © Thinkstock.

Print information available on the last page.

Rev. date: 03/12/2015

To order additional copies of this book, contact:
Xlibris
1-888-795-4274
www.Xlibris.com
Orders@Xlibris.com
700131

Contents

Statement Of Authenticity vii
Acknowledgements ix
CHAPTER 1   War Breaks Out 1
CHAPTER 2   In Transit to a Neutral Place 11
CHAPTER 3   Prisoners on a Train 13
CHAPTER 4   Kazakhstan Collective Farm 16
CHAPTER 5   A Friend of Teddy's 20
CHAPTER 6   Dr. Anna 21
CHAPTER 7   A Celebration of Amnesty 25
CHAPTER 8   Japanese Prisoners of War 28
CHAPTER 9   A New Friend Arrives 30
CHAPTER 10 An Improvement in Housing 32
CHAPTER 11 Postwar Rumors 33
CHAPTER 12 Train Ride from Kazakhstan to Poland 35
CHAPTER 13 Back in Poland Postwar 40
CHAPTER 14 Visit to Warsaw 41
CHAPTER 15 Sad News 43
CHAPTER 16 Visit to Silesia 44
CHAPTER 17 Poland to France 46
CHAPTER 18 Europe to the United States 52
CHAPTER 19 Manhattan 54

STATEMENT OF AUTHENTICITY

Stalin's Feisty Guest is as authentic as told to me by Felicia, the brave woman who lived the real life stories.

Some non-principals' names have been changed to protect their privacy.

There has been a bit of embellishment to make the stories more lively and readable. But for the most part, the stories are true to the woman who lived the stories. They are the history of part of her life.

There have been thousands of books written about the World War II era, but I found ***Gulag*** by Anne Applebaum to be an especially informative resource in my research about Soviet work camps.

ACKNOWLEDGEMENTS

This book is dedicated to Felicia, the best of storytellers, who saved her son, Teddy, from the war.

At a later time, Teddy would become the dearest person in my life. Teddy was a witness to many of the events in his mother's life which are presented in this book.

I have written this account of her life as she told it to me and as she lived it. She wanted her story to be known. One can encounter terrible events and survive them with courage and determination. Felicia did!

Thanks to my daughter, Jennifer, and my son, Michael.

I am grateful to my nephew, Chris McGee, for my book cover illustration.

I appreciate my writer friends: Karen G., Marilyn J., Donna B., Denise B., and the late Ike I.

Thank you to my friend Jan J. M. for her helpful ideas for the book.

CHAPTER 1

War Breaks Out
Warsaw, Poland and In Transit
September 1939

Felicia, Szymon, and Teddy

Teddy and Szymon

Teddy and Szymon

Teddy as Baby

Teddy as Child

Teddy with Nurse

Szymon Military Photo

It was deceptively calm before the nightmarish twist of fate began.

On the road to a summer house outside Warsaw she had rented for the summer before war broke out, Felicia spied a gypsy. The Romany fortune-teller put her long gifted sensitive fingers on the forehead of Felicia's three-year-old son. The gypsy measured Teddy's forehead and declared the child musically talented and intelligent. Felicia believed the woman's latter pronouncement. With regard to musical ability, the child had always wakened with a song. Teddy turned his head to watch and hear the gypsy disappear down the dirt road, her hands and ankles covered with jingling bells.

A phone call from her father alerted Felicia that she should return to her Warsaw apartment. There were war rumors. Her husband, Dr. Simon, a physician and reserve officer in the Polish army, was now on full military duty. The road to the summer house was almost deserted. An elderly couple offered a ride to Warsaw. She expressed her gratitude by giving the woman a ring.

Safely back in her home in the wee hours, Felicia settled the sleeping Teddy when an ominous signal began to sound. This was the sound of enemy planes. Her son, in his toddler innocence, asked about the alarm sound. Felicia made a difficult situation milder to her son than reality required. Felicia uttered, "The sound is a kitten."

The child requested, "When is the kitten coming back? I like the kitten."

Felicia knew the cellar to be the safest place; however, she remained on her second floor of the apartment to stay cozy and comfortable as long as possible.

Suddenly, her uniformed husband Simon arrived at the apartment. Simon was accompanied by an elderly man, a superior officer who looked dignified but frightened. He seemed to be clinging to Simon for dear life. Simon directed his wife to prepare their child and herself to flee from the active war. He had a plan.

As Felicia awakened and dressed the child in the early morning, a rough motor announced the military vehicle that waited to take mother and child out of harm's way. There were others in the vehicle and an orderly to help the women and children.

The terrifying news flooded their minds: the Germans were on the periphery of Warsaw. That brutal force might have entered at any moment.

Felicia gathered some gold coins and jewelry and placed them in a small strongbox. She then ran to the basement and buried the treasure in the dirt floor.

Her father phoned. "It is war, daughter!" The connection then was broken forever.

Felicia found a packet of flour and sugar that had been left by her loving father earlier for her need.

Felicia and Simon bundled their half-asleep child into the military vehicle. As Felicia, Teddy, and the others pulled away from the familiar apartment and street, the vehicle dodged dangerous enemy fire from above. Simon watched as the vehicle pulled away with his precious wife and child. He went back to the war front.

Enemy planes spied the military vehicle and tried to hit them. The driver pulled to the side of the road. All the passengers got out and hid as best as they could. Following this short stop, they all tumbled back into the vehicle and started out again. At a stop, an orderly with the group caught a chicken for soup for Teddy, but another bombing caused them to not linger. When they came close to the orderly's house, the man ran away to be with his family. Fortunately, another orderly in the vehicle would attend them. Finally, they began to eat cooked chicken in the privacy of a verdant forest. Even that long-awaited meal had to be abandoned as there were more bombings.

The hectic and frightening journey took Felicia and Teddy from Warsaw to a village near Lvov, a neutral city. Would they ever see their dear husband and father again? The trip removed Felicia from everyone whom she loved and cared, except for her toddler son Teddy. She hoped to always keep him nearby. Felicia would make it her life's mission to locate her beloved husband Simon.

CHAPTER 2

In Transit to a Neutral Place
Lvov, Poland, 1939–1940

The military vehicle left Felicia and Teddy near the entrance of a house where Felicia's family had friends. Felicia, with her hurriedly packed baggage, was offered lodging by the elderly couple, and she gratefully accepted their hospitality.

Teddy was most intrigued by the many precious figurines all around the house and tried to handle the treasures. Felicia felt that this intrusion on the elderly couples' lives was too much for them and asked them to arrange transportation for mother and child to Lvov.

Arriving in Lvov by a horse and cart, she found a modest apartment. Thoughts of respite from active war were substituted with concern over her husband at the war front. Her parents and brothers were in Warsaw; this caused great worry. Her father had business interests in Poland as well as Berlin. He had a great sense of humor. He and Felicia were especially close, as they shared the same jokes. Her mother, a serious-minded and excellent homemaker, gathered the family for weekly special meals at the cozy, comfortable apartment. Felicia had a sister who, with her new husband, had left Poland for a safer country. How well that those two dear to her had found a haven. She was also close to her two brothers.

As Felicia became settled in her apartment, she met a physician from Lvov. She asked if he would check her son, as the child had been tugging at one ear and had a fever as well. He agreed to this. She mentioned her husband being at the war front.

Walking to the market for provisions, Felicia almost stepped on a man selling matches sitting on the sidewalk. His coat looked ragged. As he lifted his hat and looked toward her, she realized he was her cousin, Sev.

How an educated lawyer could be so needy as to be selling matches on the street was unbelievable to her.

She asked if Sev had shelter.

He shook his head. "No."

Felicia invited him to share her small apartment, and at that kind offer, he rose from the pavement and walked straight and tall. Even with tattered clothes, he carried himself with utmost dignity.

The physician knocked at the apartment door, and Sev stood up to show respect as the doctor came into the room.

The doctor pronounced, "I see that your husband has returned from the war!"

Her head downcast, she introduced Sev to the physician. "He is my cousin." In looking more closely at Sev, the doctor noticed boils on the exposed parts of the man's skin and advised him to eat citrus fruits or citrus juice whenever possible. The condition, caused from a lack of Vitamin C, would improve with the suggested diet. A wartime shortage of citrus made the advice unhelpful.

Teddy pulled on one ear. Crankiness and feverishness described the usually healthy and cheerful child. The doctor, who had a wooden stethoscope dangling from his neck, allowed the curious child to play with the object. With soothing words, the doctor peered into the affected ear and solemnly pronounced, "The child has a very bad ear infection."

The doctor prescribed warm eardrops and a covering for the affected ear. "Keep the boy inside. Don't allow him out in the cold weather," advised the doctor. Felicia would long remember the doctor's instructions regarding Teddy's ear infection. Oh, if she only could have obeyed them all.

Sev had a night job at a candy factory. He brought many treats to Felicia and the child. Early one morning, as Sev still worked, Felicia heard a knock at the door. Felicia opened the door to a coterie of bearlike, brown-uniformed Russian soldiers who towered over her, flaunting badges of red stars—the badge of power. The petite figure of Felicia shook uncontrollably as the spokesman for the group introduced himself and informed her she was under arrest. He ordered her to pack a few things, bring her child, and come with them to the train station. She packed her meager belongings and bundled her child as best she could. She tied a scarf to cover his ears. Carrying her child, she followed the brown line of Russian soldiers. She stumbled in the darkness of early morning.

At the train station, she encountered a motley group of Russian "prisoners," all women. Polish military wives with children comprised most of the group. In the morose chill of dawn, the tears of the women mixed with the cold rain that fell.

CHAPTER 3

Prisoners on a Train
In Transit: Lvov, Poland to Kazakhstan,
Central Asia
1939–1940

The Polish army officers' wives and their children were packed into the dirty cattle car train in the grim, gray chill of early morning. The outside door slammed shut. Felicia maintained her composure by encouraging Teddy to believe that this train ride was an adventure. It was an advantage that at the age of three; he didn't remember clearly the cozy apartment, toys, and loving family left behind. He did have his mother to keep him constant company, and he enjoyed the ride. His presence helped Felicia to keep up her spirits. She had a child to save.

In the early part of the journey, Felicia worked on identification for her son. From a coarse cloth in her coat pocket, she embroidered her son's name, her maiden name, and her husband's name. She sewed the rough, makeshift badge on to Teddy's jacket.

Many of the women on the train spoke endlessly about beautiful possessions left behind. Felicia found silliness in the conversation. She believed that she would never see the treasures left behind in her apartment again. She hoped desperately for news of her husband.

As her child slept on her shoulder, Felicia fell asleep and dreamed of a past joyful train ride. Her new husband, Simon, had planned the trip.

For a holiday present, Simon had given Felicia a package trip to the Zakopane resort. Zakopane, located in Southern Poland, on the border with Czechoslovakia, was the scene of idyllic alpine scenery and excellent skiing. Additionally, there was an excuse not to attend the wedding of a cousin, of whom Felicia was not fond.

Upon boarding the train, bags were loaded, and soon blurred black and white countryside images were viewed. The train moved like a giant hooded serpent, tunneling in slithering waves through rock tunnels to the area close to the snow-covered summit. The train riders admired the view as high peaks came into focus.

Greeted by a horse-drawn sleigh, Felicia and Simon arrived at the resort.

The couple inhaled smells of wood fires and cinnamon. A scene of couples cozily wearing woolen sweaters and sitting around the fireplace welcomed Felicia and Simon. Guests drank mulled wine, and a number of the men were smoking using curved pipes. Conversation dotted with war rumors spoiled the contentment of the moment.

A telegram from her father directed Felicia to phone him. Responding to the message, Felicia learned that her father was insistent that she attend the cousin's wedding. She was unhappy to have her bit of paradise interrupted. However, adoring and respecting her father, she told Simon that she would return to Warsaw and attend the wedding. Leaving her luggage behind at the resort, she returned to Warsaw. Her practical-minded mother stood with arms folded and scowled at her daughter upon learning that the luggage had been left behind. Felicia made it clear that she was returning to the resort.

Felicia attended the wedding festivities and, in the process, charmed her father's side of the family. Samuel was a little surprised at his daughter's daring personality, but he was proud of her great energy and glad that she respected his wish to attend the wedding. He sent her back to the resort and rewarded her by slipping a first-class ticket in her hand for the return to Simon and fun.

Felicia was roughly awakened by the loud boots of the gruff Russian soldiers, who paraded loudly and arrogantly up and down the aisles.

When asked about the train's destination, the soldiers responded with, "We are taking you to be with your husbands."

One crude Russian commander laughed and coughed out, "If you don't find your husbands, you'll get new ones!"

Felicia cringed and tears filled her eyes. In fairness to the Russians, they didn't single out racial or religious groups to annihilate. Roughness and crudeness characterized the way the Russians in authority treated one another and everyone else. The hard life of Mother Russia's citizens didn't yield great refinement. However, children were valued greatly and treated kindly.

Scenery from the train showed constant fir tree forests dotted with small gingerbread-appearing cottages. The wooden log houses were mostly brown accented with bright colors and decals. The weather was bleak and cold. The prisoners subsisted on rations of bread, water, potatoes, cabbage, and beets. Hot water was passed out for tea.

Finally, after a long journey, the train stopped, and all passengers were harshly ordered to depart the train.

Would the women find their husbands?

CHAPTER 4

Kazakhstan Collective Farm
World War II

The long cattle car train ride ended at a Russian prison camp in Kazakhstan, Central Asia. Felicia knew her life would never be as it had been before war broke out. She was in the middle of nowhere. None of the Polish women, including Felicia, found their husbands at the journey's end. The Russian soldiers' promises were a cruel trick played on the women to keep them compliant.

Felicia, now a guest of Stalin, settled with Teddy in crude barracks with other women and children on a collective farm, one of a large number of Stalin's pet projects. There would be jobs for all captives on the farm.

The only good thing about life in Kazakhstan was that her son would always be near. A bountiful crop in the area was hay. The extremes of weather produced hot summers and cold winters. The area was known as "The Steppe of Hunger". A small river ran through the village, but water needed to be imported.

The group of Polish prisoners came under the supervision of Commander Ivan, a rough peasant who had been suddenly promoted to help in Stalin's plan for this collective farm.

Ivan proclaimed, "Jobs match skills of the prisoners!" What a cruel joke!

Felicia showed up for her work and was ushered to a muddy corral. There, a bareback ox awaited her to climb atop and lead the beast around a ring covered with manure and straw in order to make material for crude building blocks. With a lack of good wood for shelter construction, this method had been designed for the building projects. Felicia had no previous experience working with animals. She knew the job left her at great risk of developing tetanus. She trembled with fear when one of the brutes hoisted her atop the ox. Being petite, her legs were too short to hold to the creature securely, and she kept sliding off the animal. Commander Ivan shook his fist at Felicia.

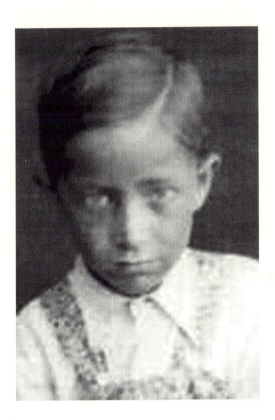

Teddy in Russia

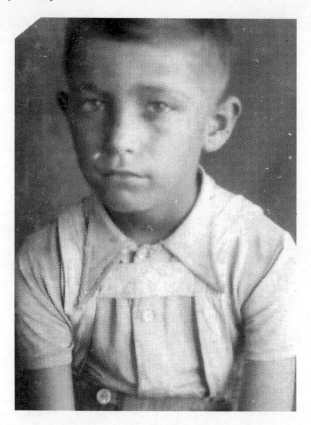

Teddy in Russia

Ivan bellowed, "You are the worst worker with the bull I have ever seen!"

Felicia snapped back, "Can you write a letter in English or French?"

Ivan screeched, "I can't read or write in Russian!"

Felicia yelled out from her perch high on the ox, "Well, I can!"

Commander Ivan informed Felicia she would have a new job of keeping statistics for the collective farm. Her new task was indeed a promotion from riding the bull.

Unfortunately, Felicia's happiness at attaining the new job was overshadowed by the earthy Commander Ivan, who informed her he expected a big bribe in return for granting her the statistics job. "I want a man's suit and watch!"

He said he planned to visit her barracks later.

Darkness fell, and only yellow animal eyes could be seen at the camp's perimeter. Ivan pounded with his fist on the door and demanded, "Let me in. You owe me a favor. I want a suit and watch!"

The women who shared the barracks helped Felicia in stacking heavy bunk beds and trunks against the door. Dogs barked. The uproar disturbed the otherwise tranquil night. The shouting and pounding became more infrequent and feeble. Ivan was unable to keep his appointment.

Felicia had no items to grant Ivan in his request for a payoff. Fortunately, shortly after this incident, superior officials transferred Ivan to another camp, far away from Felicia.

Some of the fellow prisoners poked fun at Felicia when she spoke gently to Teddy and expected him to use good manners. A woman of a coarse nature echoed the consensus held by many in the camp as she scolded and shook her fist at Felicia, "Why do you speak that way, foolish woman? You and your child will never get out of here to use such fine manners!"

Felicia ignored the comment from others whose attitudes were from feelings of despair and defeat. She believed that one day the Kazakhstan experience would be in the past.

Felicia bravely wrote a letter to Stalin to whom she voiced dissatisfaction with her present straits. She pleaded, "I am in this country against my will. I want to leave and find my husband. Please let me go back to Poland!"

She never received a formal reply from the Kremlin. This was without a doubt a good thing.

CHAPTER 5

A Friend of Teddy's
Kazakhstan, Central Asia
World War II

Katya, a blonde, rosy-cheeked Shirley Temple lookalike, was Teddy's schoolmate and the daughter of a Russian soldier. She spent time with Felicia and other camp friends. The mother, an important Communist party official, had a facial expression of stone and spoke very little to the Polish prisoners.

Katya's father, Igor, wounded in war, returned to the village by train. Katya and Teddy sat at the feet of Igor as he told stories about seeing magic hot water running from pipes inside a house. This seemed such a contrast to their present primitive living conditions. Everyone drew water from a well, and people had to heat this on a stove. The child questioned Felicia about the stories of life outside Russia.

Felicia told Katya, "People don't live with such luxuries." Felicia believed the child would never live outside that small and primitive village; she didn't want her to feel denied. What the child wouldn't know she would never miss.

Katya and Teddy were enrolled in a Russian school. Along with reading, writing, and arithmetic, the teachers taught that Lenin or Stalin created the world's important inventions. Teddy was not taken in by the propaganda. Katya believed it all.

A few months later, Felicia learned the mother of Katya had lost her good job in the Communist hierarchy. Perhaps the tales told by Igor of life in other countries had been used against him and his family.

CHAPTER 6

Dr. Anna
Kazakhstan, Central Asia
World War II

Dr. Anna, a Polish physician and fellow camp prisoner, had a great influence on Felicia's emotional and physical health. Dr. Anna's husband, a Polish physician, had been conscripted into the Polish Army, like Felicia's husband. Anna and Felicia had much in common. Dr. Anna had also been taken prisoner by Russian soldiers along with her teenage son and daughter, and she was also taken to the Kazakhstan camp. Dr. Anna's razor-sharp wit and optimism kept the spirits of her fellow camp friends in a good state.

Felicia first met Dr. Anna early in the Kazakhstan years, when there was a staccato knocking at the front door of a hut where Felicia and Teddy lived under the auspices of a Kazakh peasant couple soon after Felicia had been promoted to keeping camp statistics. A petite dark blonde with sparkling brown eyes appeared. She related that as she slept, her clothes had been stolen. Although the garments were crammed beneath her pillow for safekeeping, a crafty thief used a stick to pry the clothing from the hiding place. Dr. Anna implored, "Would you have any clothing I might borrow so that I can go to work?" The doctor had gone from hut to hut to obtain any items others might spare in her emergency. Felicia proceeded to gather things she could spare and later saw the doctor wearing a jumble of varied sizes, colors, and both men's and women's clothing to put together an outfit. The coterie of captives gazed at the crazy quilt of attire, including a man's hat jammed on Dr. Anna's head that caused her hair to peek out untidily in all directions, as the doctor laughed and joked about the theft.

Felicia and Dr. Anna became great friends. Felicia asked Dr. Anna if they would come out of this traumatic life experience as normal people.

Dr. Anna responded, "Not completely!" However, she believed that Teddy, at his very young age, would do well, as he had little memory of all he had left behind in the way of loved ones and the cozy apartment. He had a good foundation of nutrition and medical care in the very early years. Now he had his mother's attentive devotion.

Dr. Anna was pleased to practice medicine in the camp, although upon her arrival she was refused permission to work by Russian officials. General paranoia among those in charge led the captors to be fearful of captive doctors. Feeling that the doctors might try to extract revenge on the captors was the root of the anxiety. Chronic shortages of Russian doctors, however, forced the officials to allow Dr. Anna to work. As remuneration for her task, she received surplus food.

Dr. Anna had an outrageous sense of humor. She passed out recipes for goodies that the camp friends hadn't eaten in months and were sure they wouldn't have again. Treats such as apple strudel and other tasty baked goods were part of her recipe campaign.

Dr. Anna risked severe punishment when she cared for an ill Felicia. Frightening rumors of a typhus epidemic became rampant in the camp. The diagnosis of typhus or another contagious disease was to lead to quarantine, and usually the patient was taken to a crowded hospital with primitive and unsanitary treatment. Few survived such poor care. The illness was to be reported to authorities by the doctor; if not, there were severe penalties. Dr. Anna didn't report the typhus diagnosis even after Felicia broke out in a classic typhus rash. Dr. Anna chose to take care of Felicia by herself. The doctor would come to Felicia's hut early, before the doctor was to go to work, check the stove fire, give her friend a sponge bath, fix a meal, and prepare Teddy for school. The kind physician would take Teddy to school. Fortunately, Felicia made a full recovery.

Dr. Hertzog also came down with typhus and, fortunately, also recovered well. Dr. Hertzog reported the diagnosis of rheumatoid arthritis as the reason for her and Felicia being ill. It was accepted by the authorities.

Dr. Anna asked Felicia to accompany her on childbirth cases. Little, if any, prenatal care existed. Many mothers and babies died due to a lack of technology in Central Asia. Women took pride in many pregnancies. Those prolific women often received medals from the government to honor their fertility. Children were an asset to farms and, in line with Stalin's plans, were a boon to the growth of Communism.

Felicia's thoughts took her back to her own son's birth in Poland. She and Simon were happy when their newborn child Teddy was born. With her outrageous wit, she joked to her proper obstetrician, "He has red hair. I don't want a red-haired child. Take him away!"

"I'll take him. I have four daughters," bantered the doctor. Humor was Felicia's way of dealing with highly charged emotional times. A superstition from the European old wives' tales at that time expressed that one should never show too much joy over offspring as "the angels might hear this boasting and become jealous." Bragging may bring bad luck.

The entire family was pleased with Teddy. A woman from the country was employed to live with their family; she was to care for the baby and to be a wet nurse.

What a contrast—to see the primitive childbirth conditions in wartime Russia compared with that of pre-war Poland! The women in Kazakhstan usually gave birth in mud-floored huts, and there was little good food, water, or medical care to be found. Back in Poland, Felicia had a good obstetrician and a cozy hospital experience, and she was supported by her loving family.

Dr. Anna and Felicia did knitting for the Russian army. The women worked until the wee hours by kerosene lamp to make the deadline of a certain number of two- or three-fingered gloves that enabled soldiers to hold their rifles.

An elderly man, a doctor from Moscow, had visited the women and told of his life. The conversations were enjoyed by Felicia and Anna. They loved stories. However, one day the doctor was taken for interrogation and asked why he visited the women. Unmonitored conversations were not permitted. He never again visited the women.

In World War II Russia, money had little or no value. Dr. Anna, Felicia, and other camp friends survived economically by bartering. Felicia had a considerable amount of clothing. Russians valued European garments. The items could be traded for food or other necessities.

In the village, people wishing to barter could go weekly to an area to exchange items. Individuals displayed their wares, and one could approach those who had things to trade and freely exchange goods.

One day at the bartering place, a high Russian official's wife, Nadia, approached Felicia, who dangled a pair of antelope-skin shoes. The fancy shoes were tied together and swinging from Felicia's shoulders in an effort to display them. Nadia wanted to take the shoes and told Felicia she'd trade the shoes for an agreed amount of flour that Felicia needed badly. Felicia could live well without the fancy custom-made shoes and agreed on the offer as Nadia snatched away the footwear.

Felicia showed up at Nadia's house to get the flour.

Nadia screamed, "You get no flour. If you come back, I will set my dogs on you!" Felicia saw a number of growling, snarling dogs!

Sweet revenge happened when the deceitful Nadia tried a similar one-way barter on Dr. Anna over an exchange of a suit of the good doctor for Nadia's potatoes. The potatoes turned out to be rotten.

Dr. Anna pronounced to Nadia, "I am a witch. I put a curse on you!"

Months later, Felicia and Dr. Anna learned that Nadia's daughter died of tuberculosis. Nadia's husband was caught stealing and sentenced to prison. The disreputable Nadia disappeared from the village.

CHAPTER 7

A Celebration of Amnesty Post Hitler's Invasion of Russia World War II

In 1941, Hitler's armies stormed across Russian borders, cracking the non-aggression treaty crafted by Stalin's and Hitler's diplomats, Molotov and von-Ribbentrop. This event caused the Russian government to grant an amnesty agreement, giving the Polish prisoners freedom; it was an astonishing event. Initially, the Polish people, enemies of Germany, had been automatically enemies of Russia as well. Overnight, Felicia and her camp friends were considered enemies of the Russians no more. In the context of the way the Russian government would treat eastern European citizens under their control in future Cold War times, this was an amazing milestone. Within the Russian territory, the poorly-prepared German army would be defeated by the Russian army in many horrific battles. The Russian people would have horrible lives during this time.

Felicia and Teddy were now living under the protection of a Kazakh couple on the edge of town not far from the work camp in a building made of mud construction. A stream ran in front of the house; there were often rains in the spring that made the water rise and become a gushing torrent. Steppeland was beyond the mud hut. Felicia rented a room in the mud building. The accommodation consisted of a bed and small cot that was in a part of the kitchen and if not luxurious was at least cozy and warm. The occupants of the house drew water from a well. Kerosene lamps were used in the evening. There was no electricity.

A partially enclosed area in a courtyard held chickens that were kept by the Kazakh family. Teddy, recovering from diphtheria, often sat outside in the sun, observing the chickens. He noticed that when the mother hen had a new chick, she would shoo away her previous brood, rejecting those from the old brood; the rejection of the old chicks was an interesting observation to Teddy.

As war broke out in Poland, Felicia's brother, Stasiek, searching for a neutral place, had been grabbed by Russian military, transported to Russian territory, and sentenced to slave labor in Siberia. With other Polish citizens, in an astonishing change of fate due to the amnesty, Stasiek was let out of the labor camp and told he was now free! Amazingly, Stasiek was told the whereabouts of his sister, and after a journey to Kazakhstan, he suddenly showed up at the mud house of the Kazakh couple.

Stasiek told of his plan to join with other Polish men to fight the enemies in a Polish free army after an uneasy truce between Stalin and Polish officials-in-exile created the army. Stalin had decided to utilize his former enemies (the Polish male captives) to fight the mutual fascist enemies. Officials for this Polish-in-exile army would be located in England, but Stasiek and other men willing to fight would go where they were needed.

Seeing Felicia's brother created a cheerful time. The jubilant group sat around the kitchen table and watched the fire in the fireplace dance and sputter. Fond of her tenants, the Kazakh woman displayed her treat of sausage and pickles.

As a treat upon his arrival at the landlord of Felicia, Stasiek brought a gift of a bottle of vodka that he had obtained by bartering. The Kazakh landlord's eyes sparkled as he spied the diamond clear bottle. As if enchanted, he held the cylindrical item, gently caressed its hourglass form, and announced, "Tonight we celebrate the arrival of Felicia's brother and his freedom from the Siberian labor camp!" The Kazakh woman appeared with her treasured set of shot glasses she had bought at a fair years before. The landlord insisted on a marathon of upturned glasses.

Glassy-eyed, the landlord turned to Felicia and tilted his elf-like pink head toward Teddy. "The reason you Poles can't drink is that you never started young enough." He proceeded to snatch the child from Felicia's arms against her protests. He threatened Felicia with the choice of a bed out of doors if she refused to comply with his demands. The landlord then poured a shot glass of vodka and offered this to the child who coughed and made a choking sound.

Felicia trembled with fear. "You'll kill my child!" After the drink, the child fell asleep, and Felicia took him in her arms Pieta-like and carried the limp child to his cot.

The next morning, Teddy was too still with a high fever. His speech sounded incoherent. Felicia was very frightened and sent her brother to the town to summon a Polish physician.

A woman doctor rushed in, and, upon recognizing Felicia as an old schoolmate from Poland, exclaimed, "Felka, Felka!" She was Dr. Helena, who called Felicia by her childhood nickname. The doctor unbuttoned Teddy's shirt and noticed that the child was peppered with a red rash. She identified the child's illness as Asian measles. Felicia was so relieved that her child recovered from the doses of vodka! For a time, she feared that the vodka had killed him.

For the Kazakhstan camp prisoners, the first good result of the amnesty was that they would all have improved living conditions. Felicia and Teddy would soon share a house with Dr. Anna and her teenage children.

Following a Kazakhstan stay, Stasiek would join the Polish Free Army and eventually, with other Polish troops, would fight courageously in Italy under British leadership.

CHAPTER 8

Japanese Prisoners of War
Ayaguz, Russia
World War II

Obsessed with the thought of reuniting with her husband and remaining hopeful, Felicia frequently walked to the railroad station, the center of any news from the war front. Any train that traversed this isolated part of the Soviet Union stopped at Ayaguz, the closest village from the camp. Felicia and other wives waited for any scrap of news about Simon and other husbands' regiments. Any civilians, prisoners, or military personnel were required to make a stop at the train station.

Simon's regiment, she learned, had been captured and classified as a prisoner of war unit. At least hope existed for Simon to be alive. However, she had no information of him as an individual.

The crisscross of tracks resembled oriental characters and symbols. This prophetic clue preceded the amazing appearance of a trainload of Japanese prisoners, clad in traditional prison garb. Russians and Polish people, who wore mud-spattered garments of rough cloth, stood with mouths agape as they eyeballed the Japanese prisoners who rushed out of the train toward water pumps at the fringe of the track. With small and adept hands, the Japanese carried small basins and dumped water over themselves, each taking turns with the creaky water pump. The men washed furiously as though within the water lurked a spiritual panacea that would serve to purify their war-damaged souls. The water ritual united the Asian men.

Carrying her daily ration of coarse and grainy black bread, Felicia heard a Japanese prisoner say in Russian, "Hungry." She handed her ration to the man. The man smiled at her and handed her a fountain pen.

The pen consisted of a mother-of-pearl base with black onyx design. The pen would always be a prized possession.

The Japanese prisoners whom Felicia stared at in Kazakhstan possessed a degree of grace and dignity unlike any other prisoners of war Felicia had encountered. For years to come, she would wonder what had happened to the men, imprisoned in a land of such an alien culture, language, and values from their "Land of the Rising Sun."

CHAPTER 9

A New Friend Arrives
Post Amnesty World War II

Felicia's brother Stasiek invited a friend, Edward, who had been a fellow prisoner in Siberia and now freed, to the village in Kazakhstan.

Edward, an intelligent man, was healthy and energetic. Prior to the war, he owned a factory that manufactured clothing for working people. With rumors of impending war raging, Edward fled Poland for a safer place. Later, Edward would learn that his wife didn't survive the war. Edward soon lost his neutral haven and was grabbed by the Russian military. He became a Russian prisoner and was sent to a labor camp in Siberia, a fate that befell many other Polish citizens who left their homes in an attempt to escape the German occupation.

Soon after arriving in Kazakhstan, Edward, an enterprising person, started a haircomb factory. The chief material utilized in producing the rough combs was the horn of oxen. He pumped a foot-powered lathe, obtained from a bartering transaction. Sharp prongs were carved into the horns. His venture did not produce the success he craved; the resulting sharp edges could puncture the scalp and cause bleeding. Finally, the enterprise folded when thieves stole the remaining horns.

After heavy snow melted along railroad tracks, random bits of coal and wood could be visualized. The knotty bark of the wood peeked from the winter white and small bits of coal showed through the snow. With his business-savvy mind, Edward noticed an opportunity to provide fuel to the huts and use the items for the purpose of trading.

Edward rented a camel named Yuri from a Kazakh trader. Yuri's owner told Edward of the creature's churlish temper only after Edward had paid the fee. Following the attachment of a sled device on the camel by which to haul fuel, the journey began.

Yuri, with the lowering of his long eyelashes, seemed to convey to the temporary master, "This job is too demeaning!" For emphasis, a projectile of green cud flew out of the camel's mouth, nearly hitting Edward.

Having finished the gathering of coal and wood bits, Edward begged the camel to continue the journey along railroad tracks. By this time, the camel had eased down to slumber on a grassy slope beside the tracks. The creature's tranquility was in contrast to Edward's anger at having been unable to continue the trip. Even after he pulled a rope attached to Yuri's jaw with all his might, the animal did not move. The stubborn camel tried to pull the man, instead of the man smoothly leading the animal. People who noticed the awkward trip laughed heartily at the sight. Finally, in frustration, Edward asked a friend to go to the Kazakh trader's hut and get the owner to take Yuri home.

There were no further ventures concerning the camel, as there was too much risk involved in such a scheme. Technically, all coal on the railroad tracks belonged to the Soviet government. Edward could have been arrested for his scheme. The camel's uncooperative behavior saved Edward from an awful fate had he chosen to continue such a venture.

Edward lived on the edge. One day, on a brisk walk to the village of Ayaguz, his pocket jingled with gold coins which he had obtained from a bartering venture. Not content with his present sum, Edward hoped to take part in a black market money exchange transaction. He walked with purpose, his pockets heavy with the treasure. He whistled, smiled, and proudly patted his secret treasure. He stopped in a store to buy a samovar of tea to improve his mood and fortify him against the incessant cold wind. Unfortunately, as Edward turned in to enter the tea shop, he noticed a policeman searching people ahead to see if they carried illegal items. Quickly, Edward slid into a corner of the rustic room, removed the coins from his pocket, and swallowed them all. He grimaced as the last coin slid down his throat with great difficulty.

He later joked and laughed with his friends about the coin incident. Swallowing the coins was a lot better than having them found by the police. One could be sent to a salt mine—or worse.

Edward and Felicia became close friends. Felicia came to believe that he helped in the survival of Teddy and herself.

CHAPTER 10

An Improvement in Housing
Kazakhstan
World War II

Better housing came about after Felicia and Teddy left the kitchen quarters of the primitive dwelling of the Kazakh couple and moved to a shared house with Dr. Anna and her two precocious teenagers. An Arab man owned the house. Finally, Felicia, Teddy, and the three members of Dr. Anna's family found space for everyone.

Teddy came home from school announcing he had viewed beautiful puppies at a Russian neighbor's house. Since he had no toys, Felicia thought he deserved a puppy. Teddy picked a black dog, a mongrel, and named him Blackie.

After bringing the puppy home, Felicia managed to train him. Blackie learned not to do his business in Felicia's room, but he would do this in other rooms in the house. Teddy was very fond of the dog.

Dr. Anna's inquisitive offspring tried electrical experiments in the house. When power would go out as a result of the research, an official would show up to inquire why this happened. Dr. Anna and Felicia would pretend ignorance, as tampering with utilities was an illegal activity.

With Felicia's gift for language facility, some mothers in the village asked if she could teach an English class. Happy to do this, she didn't apply for a special permit. In order to be covered, the students held knitting projects in their laps, and in case of an unexpected visit by the dreaded secret police, there was an excuse for the gathering. The students had to obey an established rule of no locked doors.

CHAPTER 11

Postwar Rumors

Rumors were flying to the effect that the entire group would be allowed out of Russia to go back to Poland. For one to be allowed to leave Russia was almost unbelievable. The former prisoners all knew that. Lists circulated, disclosing names of persons proclaimed to stay in Russia and those who were to emigrate.

A vicious man managed to have Felicia's name placed on a list of those who were to stay. The dubious privilege of being on the "to stay" list was eligibility to vote. When Felicia didn't show up at the polling place, two burly men came for her and took her to the voting place. She was fortunately rescued by the mayor of the town, who confirmed that she was not to vote but was on a list to leave Russia.

One night Felicia received a visit from two Russian secret policemen. She was told to dress and come with them. Hurriedly donning her warmest clothing and topping her head with a kerchief, she followed the men as she stumbled in the dark. Fearing the worst, after she was offered a cigarette, she got the good news that the entire group of former prisoners would be allowed to leave and she would be the interpreter. Everyone from the group was summoned alphabetically and individually told that the person would be allowed to leave Russia soon. Felicia was seated in the office as people came in for the information about emigration permission.

As daybreak finally struck and Felicia left the officials' office, she greeted people who were ready to go to work. None answered her. She finally realized that others thought she was working with the secret police and betraying fellow former prisoners. This was not the case. She was simply helping with the transfer due to her language facility. Finally, fellow prisoners understood her role.

The prisoners were informed a train would be prepared to take them back to Poland. Teddy was unhappy when he learned that he would have to give up his dog. The Kazakh couple with whom they had shared a hut agreed to take Blackie with the agreement that Teddy would visit the dog each day. The first few days, the dog greeted Teddy in a playful way with tail wagging. After a while the dog was indifferent to visits. Felicia explained to Teddy that the dog probably found out they were leaving the village and Russia.

CHAPTER 12

Train Ride from Kazakhstan to Poland Postwar

Felicia, Teddy, and the entire group of Polish captives now had permission to leave Kazakhstan. The war was over. This group was one of the first ones to be given Stalin's consent to go back to Poland. This was an amazing event. Felicia, Teddy, and their friends from the six years in Central Asia shortly would no longer be guests of Stalin.

Teddy had grown from a toddler to a nine-year-old. He came out of the deprived experience normally, due perhaps to his early foundation of infant care, nutrition, and love. He had his mother's total attention. She expected him to use good manners. Felicia had a deep belief that one day both would leave the crude way of life. It was more difficult for the older children who remembered the cozy homes and loved ones left behind back in Poland.

Shortly before preparing for the train trip, Teddy came running to his mother after playing outside. His right arm was held high with glints of sun streaming from a metal object.

"Mama, I have money for you! Now you're rich!"

His mother asked where he had obtained the treasure of a small coin. It seemed that when picking flowers near a ditch being dug by some prisoners, one of the men asked if Teddy would get him a cup of water. The boy ran to a water well and brought the clear, wet liquid to the eager man, who gulped the drink and handed the child a coin. Teddy gripped the item tightly, and his small hands were almost purple from the pressure. Felicia put her face at her child's level, looked him straight in the eyes, and said, "Never, take money from a thirsty or a hungry person." Together, they trekked to that ditch, and in a reluctant gesture, the coin was returned to the prisoner by the boy. Teddy's hands returned to their pink color as the grip on the coin was released.

The train journey would take place in converted cattle train cars. The travelers knew the trip was to be an enormous endeavor. Kazakhstan is an enormous country. Edward hired and supervised the workmen who cut out two windows with small benches underneath. The benches were to be used as an observation post, especially for the children, to view the upcoming scenery. Nine-year-old Teddy was aware the trip would be a magnificent, once-in-a-lifetime experience with splendid views of mountains, desert flats, farms, and steppe lands. The great Volga River was to be crossed! The train would pass from Asia to the European continent. The travelers would see scenery and persons they had never seen before nor would probably ever see again. There began a frenzied baking and preparing of food. Hot water was to be purchased or obtained at certain stops. The train would not be a priority one according to the Soviet government, and would not follow a regular schedule.

Felicia, Teddy, and their close friends were given a larger-than-average railroad car due to the need for Dr. Anna to care for patients along the way. This car was provided with a table and crate for the doctor's need. As rough as this train car was, to Felicia it was beautiful. It meant that she and her son and their group would get to leave Kazakhstan.

Finally, the day arrived for the passengers to board the train that would take them on an extremely long journey. The eager passengers lined up, and all got on the locomotive.

Peeking out the windows, the train riders viewed Teddy's Russian schoolmate, Katya, and her mother walking by slowly down the road in front of the station. The woman looked straight ahead, apparently oblivious to her surroundings. There was a rag wrapped around the young girl's right arm; the hand was missing. Katya and Teddy recognized each other.

Teddy asked, "What happened to you?"

She replied, "My mother lost her job in the communist party, and now we are homeless. I burned my arm on a stove before that." Then they continued on their way.

As young as he was, Teddy was deeply impressed by this change in fortune in someone he knew.

The Kazakh couple, their former landlords, waved, and the woman wiped away tears with her apron. They had brought Blackie, Teddy's former pet dog, who looked up at the train window. Teddy waved at the dog.

As the train began to pull out of the Ayaguz railroad station, the group of former captives witnessed roving gangs of ill-clad, dirty ruffians, whose threatening presence increased collective unease aboard the train. The unruly lot of boys walked with menacing looks and uplifted arrogant heads until a Communist party official passed, at which time one lad bowed low and rushed to pick up a paper dropped by the official. Felicia and Teddy learned that the poor, undisciplined fellows were war orphans.

The train arrived at its first stop, Alma-Ata, Kazakhstan's capital city. In 1997 Astana became the new capital city. The travelers had a look at the splendidly snow-capped Ala-Tau mountain range, as well as fir trees in the foreground. The Polish train riders were allowed to be out of the train for a time. They beheld some very interesting faces. Many people appeared to have been descended from the Mongol Emperor Genghis Khan, with their high cheekbones and mysterious almond-shaped dark eyes. The Asian-Kazakhstan natives stared at the Polish travelers. The rail passengers could hardly wait to breathe the air of a different place from that where they had been cooped up for six years! Everything looked and smelled so clean. They felt they were getting a taste of freedom!

Felicia and Teddy walked around Alma-Ata. At a juice vendor's stand, both tasted the most delicious fruit drink they would ever experience. An aid organization that helped the émigrés donated money so that the newly freed persons could have a good meal. Teddy refused to attend this meal due to his shyness. Felicia brought her son his food wrapped in a cloth. He ate his meal on the train. They were back on the train to continue the journey.

The first day out of Alma-Ata, wild strawberries were spotted not far from the tracks. The train made a stop, and although it was tempting for a rider to get out and pick berries, this was felt to be a poor idea. One had no idea how long the train would be stopped. However, the riders yearned for treats like the strawberries.

The monotony of the flat desert dominated the scenery as the train hugged the land. In the early journey, omnipresent images of the vastness of the arid desert and glimpses of workers planting on scant patches of soil in areas of collective farms met the eyes of passengers. Farmers walked with camels that balked at their loads. Packs of wild horses raced, leaving trails in the wake. Felicia and her fellow travelers were desperate for water to relieve their parched throats. Voices croaked due to the lack of moisture in the vocal cords. Rumors circulated that water at the upcoming station was too dangerous to drink. This unfortunate development could not have happened at a less opportune time.

In order to attain a safe supply of water, the train drew closer to the City of Thieves, an infamous site where it was rumored the current inhabitants were descendants of a lost tribe of stealers. The residents of this notorious hamlet would ply their stealing trade on unwary travelers who had the misfortune to stop at the village's tracks.

The train stopped at the town, and the group of friends took turns keeping watch over valuable items or personal articles. It was a warm evening, and all of the train windows were open. Thieves outside the train attached hooks to lines in an attempt to pick up train riders' valuables. Some of the thieves were on top of the train trying to put fishing lines and hooks down gaps in the car's ceiling to retrieve small items. Edward foiled the robbing plans by grabbing a knife and cutting all of the lines in the car. Soon, there was heard the sound of cursing and fast muffled feet rushing away in the darkness. Finally, water was loaded on the train, and the locomotive continued its journey.

While crossing from Asia to Europe, Felicia, Dr. Anna, Edward, and a man from another railroad car played bridge. It got very late. The extra man went to his own car. In the morning, the three friends looked for the extra bridge player and were surprised to find that the man's car had gotten separated from their own car. Felicia and her friends never again saw the man. They had started a bridge game in Asia and ended the game in Europe.

A change in continents occurred when the Ural Mountains appeared, indicating the division of land and people that had long existed. The Urals are the boundary between Asia and Europe.

To Teddy, the most important part of the trip was when the train crossed the enormous Volga River. Teddy insisted that he was to be awakened if the Volga crossing happened at night. Alas, Teddy fell asleep, and Felicia decided not to awaken him as the huge locomotive accelerated over the Volga River at night. As it bisected the river, the powerful locomotive seemed minute in comparison with the mighty Volga expanse. The river symbolized the strength of the Russian people. A feeling of warmth enveloped the train riders who perceived the Volga as a nurturing mother. They were as children, soothed by the mother's heartbeat, yet saddened as they absorbed and felt her pain and grief. The moon cast shots of light on the enormous inky river. Through a foggy mist, the lights on a gathering of barges resembled cathedral candles topped with haloes. Finally, rays of dawn guided the train out of that unforgettable and mysterious journey. The train riders were on their way to freedom!

The train finally reached the Polish border. This turned out to be a dangerous time for the Polish people, who suddenly became immigrants within their own country. Some extreme Polish partisans blamed the train group for their own deprivation and threatened to shoot them on sight. At the train station, the Red Cross arrived to help with food, blankets, and money. The persons on the train were sorely lacking all basic goods. Partisans were shooting wildly at the train car. Fortunately, no passengers were hit. After what Felicia and her camp friends had gone through, it was a sad situation to have such a greeting.

The train stopped at the city of Lublin. There would be money given by the aid organization at the stop to pay for food and other items. Felicia understood that the train was to be at that stop for a long time. However, when she returned to the train, it had vanished along with her son and her friends. She started to cry. Her body was shaking. Finally, she learned that another train was arriving that would hook up with the original train.

More composed, Felicia got on the second train and happily spied the familiar car with her son and her friends. The trains hooked up. Then she saw Teddy.

Teddy told his mother, "I wasn't worried at all!"

Finally, after six years, Felicia was no longer Stalin's guest. She realized soon after her arrival back in severely war-damaged Poland that being Stalin's guest had in all likelihood saved her life and her son's life as well.

Teddy never forgot that his mother allowed him to sleep during the Volga River crossing. He believed that he was cheated from a once-in-a-lifetime experience.

CHAPTER 13

Back in Poland Postwar 1945

The new arrivals, now back in Poland, were not prepared for the severely war-damaged country that sadly greeted them.

The city of Breslau (Wroclaw) was the city of destination for Felicia, Teddy, and Edward. The city's ancient buildings were mostly destroyed. As a direct result of fighting during World War II, most of its residential and industrial areas were heavily damaged or entirely destroyed.

Some buildings had been spared. However, many showed halves of bathrooms with exposed fixtures. The half-rooms appeared vulnerable, like a medical school skeleton that dangled for all to see.

Teddy, upon arrival at Breslau, blurted out, "What an awful smell!" A dreadful pungent odor permeated the air.

His elders responded, "It is the smell of death."

Before and during most of World War II, most of the occupants of Breslau were German. The occupants either fled or were pushed out by Allied troops during 1944-1945.

Thereafter, most of the population became Polish.

CHAPTER 14

Visit to Warsaw
Postwar

A need to close the circle of Felicia's long and ambivalent journey back to Poland was an impetus to visit her old apartment. She took a train by herself from Breslau to Warsaw. On the once familiar street where she and Simon had lived so happily during their marriage, she spied an old lamp post. Now, the post was askew. Its dignity was lost, as if pushed over by a careless giant. The former tidy neighborhood was now littered with loose bricks. Dirty boards were piled up. Dust and dirt were everywhere. Suddenly, a rat scurried, arrogantly grabbing a morsel of bread close to Felicia's feet. Felicia shuddered. In front of the falling-down building that once had been her beautiful apartment and her husband's office, she noticed the brass nameplate that remained attached to the front door. Scrawled in rough writing was an unfamiliar name.

Summoning all of her courage with posture erect, she knocked at the front door. This had been the office part of her former dwelling. It appeared that the living quarters had been damaged and now was not habitable.

A disheveled-appearing woman showing rumpled hair opened the door a bit. She peered out, blinking like a disturbed owl showing unfocused eyes that were close together. The woman inquired in a low, rough voice in Polish, "Who are you and what do you want?"

Felicia told the woman that she had a very good friend who lived at this apartment before the war. The woman beckoned her to come in. She turned her back, and Felicia could view a crude stove set up in the former doctor office of Felicia's husband. The air hung stagnant with the smell of cabbage cooking. The only familiar view to Felicia was the wallpaper, a floral pattern formerly fresh, bright, and new that Felicia had picked out as a new bride. Now, that paper was of a dingy yellow cast; the flowers on the paper looked faded and dead.

Memories surfaced, bringing back a happy and interesting time. Seeing that wallpaper reminded Felicia of a day years ago when she was helping her husband as a receptionist in this very room. An older woman with a scarlet dress arrived at Simon's office. She wore a gold charm bracelet that clinked and clanked. The woman compulsively took her long white gloves off and put them back on. She announced herself as Madame Natralova and insisted that she must see the doctor. Refusing to state her business, it was assumed that she had a health problem. Ushered in by Felicia, Madame Natralova entered the inner sanctum of Simon's office. However, in a reflex action, after only a few moments, Simon brusquely ushered the woman back to the reception area. Madame Natralova's business turned out to be that of a marriage broker who hoped to enlist Simon as a client. Upon the matrimonial agent's final haughty departure, Felicia received an ill-tempered scowl from the woman, as if the matchmaker blamed the wife for the loss of a possible commission.

In the present time, Felicia knew she had to get out of the room or she would faint. She walked backwards to the doorknob that led to the hall. She remembered she had hidden a strongbox in the basement of the building just before her journey away from the war. In great haste, a hole had been dug in the dirt floor, and she had placed the box which contained some gold jewelry and other small treasures in the hiding place. Could the items still be there? The valuables could prove useful to her future needs.

Felicia raced down the steep dark basement steps to run straight into a huge, rough- looking fellow with a dirty gray beard and piercing eyes. The coarse man lurked behind the immense and noisy water boiler. He smoked and gestured with a long-handled wooden pipe. Ash and fire spewed out of the pipe like a volcanic eruption. He coughed out a brief query in Polish, "What are you doing here?"

"I took the wrong turn," Felicia said as she ran up the cellar stairs to the outdoors and never looked back.

Felicia never returned to that former haven, now an unpleasant, unwelcome, and even a possibly dangerous place for her.

CHAPTER 15

Sad News
Postwar

Felicia learned that her husband Simon had been killed, along with thousands of other Polish military officers, in a massacre at the now infamous Katyn Forest near Smolensk.

When the mass graves were initially unearthed, leaders of the Russian military blamed the massacre on the German Army, or Wehrmacht. Such an explanation seemed credible to many due to the egregious numbers of other Nazi wartime atrocities. As more facts came out, however, it was discovered that this war crime had indeed been committed by the Soviet Union, under direct orders from Stalin's chief lieutenant, Beria. The Soviet Union's role in this notorious event was not officially acknowledged by the Kremlin until the Gorbachev era.

Soviet attitudes toward prisoners of war were cruel and barbaric. According to Stalin, they were traitors—and those ideas extended to their own POWs.

Political motivations also played a key role in the killings at Katyn. Stalin and Beria saw many of the Polish military leaders as possible threats to post-war Soviet influence in Poland and ensured these possible nuisances would not be around to challenge the Communist regime's domination.

Today Simon's name is on a list of Polish military officers, termed by post-war Poles "the flowers of Poland," who were massacred at Katyn.

Throughout the Cold War period, Polish people recalled the Katyn Forest tragedy as a vital and symbolic reminder of Soviet ruthlessness and oppression.

CHAPTER 16

Visit to Silesia

Felicia, Teddy, and Edward visited Dr. Anna, her husband, and her two children in their new house in Silesia. The house that went with the newly released husband's position was beautiful and spacious and filled with antiques. The house originally had been snatched from innocent victims. Prior to the family being granted the house, enemy tenants were evicted and arrested by the allies. Clothes still warm from enemy tenants consisted of fine dresses and fur coats.

The outcome of World War II had a happy ending for the family of Dr. Anna, as all were united. The fact that Dr. Anna's husband survived the war was a miracle in itself. He had been head of a neurology department before the war. During the war, he was held in a prisoner-of-war camp in Hungary and was not allowed to practice medicine. He tried every possible means to practice even without pay just to keep up his skills; he was denied even this meager opportunity. One night, a highly respected citizen of the town in Hungary, a member of the aristocracy, walked past the camp and became acutely ill. The doctor was summoned and asked to take care of the count, saving the man's life. The count felt indebted to the doctor and presented to the doctor the distinguished title "groff" as was to be before the doctor's name from then on. The count used his influence to allow the doctor to practice medicine.

One evening, the count invited the doctor to his mansion for dinner. For a dessert course, a pear with a silver knife and fork was presented. The guests proceeded to eat the pear by first peeling off the skin.

The doctor looked around at the group and at first didn't eat the pear, saying, "I don't take skin off pears, as that part of the pear contains vitamins." He then took up the pear in his hands and, in front of the elegant company, proceeded to eat the fruit, skin and all.

The count followed the doctor's lead, and others at the table followed this custom. This became the count's custom from then on.

During the visit of Felicia, Edward, and Teddy, Dr. Anna, in her humorous, outrageous way, modeled the high style clothing. This was a crazy contrast to the time in the camp when she had created a motley collection of clothing gathered from various camp friends after her own clothes had been stolen from a hiding place under her pillow.

Dr. Anna had passed out recipes of delicious pastries in the camp when there were no ingredients available to make the goodies—another facet of her hilarious side.

During the visit, Dr. Anna actually served a delicious kuchen, a cake from a recipe she had passed out during the years when Felicia and Dr. Anna were camp friends. The cake, loaded with butter, sugar, and eggs (all items that had been at a dearth in Kazakhstan), melted in their mouths.

Felicia, Teddy, and Edward were glad to witness the reunion of the brave family and to have a glimpse of their happiness after Dr. Anna and her husband had been through such difficult times.

CHAPTER 17

Poland to France Postwar

After less than a year, Felicia left her native country for a hopefully better life in France. Her uncle Maurice, a Parisian, agreed to sponsor the trio of Felicia, Teddy, and Edward. The three took a second-class train from Warsaw to Paris. In Prague, Czechoslovakia, during a long, scheduled stop, they weren't allowed to leave the train station. An organization gave each of the émigrés on the train food in a station restaurant. Teddy, sensitive about strangers observing him eating, refused to go to the café. Felicia carried food wrapped in a cloth to her son.

Felicia's uncle Maurice and his wife met them at the Paris station. What a good sight for Felicia to see close family again. Displaced persons had to be vouched for by a relative. France didn't want immigrants draining the economy in an already fragile time.

The newcomers learned from a family friend, a witness to wartime events, that Uncle Maurice and his close family escaped from harm's way by a thread in occupied Paris. The family prepared to leave for the south of France to find safety. Their daughter Helena hadn't arrived home from school. The two waited anxiously. Finally, the daughter arrived, and as the three scrambled into a waiting car, they spied a gendarme at their door. They sped off. Later, they learned that the policeman queried a neighbor, as the official clutched a list with the family name, including orders to bring the family to the police station. The neighbor gave no clue about the whereabouts of the family.

Uncle Maurice owned a successful knitwear business. The neighbor then went about hiding Maurice's machinery for the business in a nearby barn. The official was unsuccessful in his quest. The family arrived at their destination in the south of France where they lived safely during the war.

The grateful Maurice, able to resume the business after he came out of hiding after the war, was forever indebted to the friend.

Open house at Uncle Maurice's, a weekly occurrence, brought many friends and relatives to rejoice at the end of such difficult times. The uncle offered to give Felicia a monthly allowance so that she might empower herself. She turned this down. "I am too young. I have skills. I will get a job."

Felicia's French relatives thought she looked older than she should. She attributed the skin damage to the years in Kazakhstan. Maria, a friend of the family who worked for a cosmetics firm, arrived at one of the family parties with a large basket for Felicia. The basket was overflowing with face creams and assorted cosmetics. Felicia had her self-esteem lifted when she realized the interest others were taking in her renewal.

In order to attend school, Teddy needed a birth certificate. Teddy's had been destroyed during the war. Felicia went to a judge who told her that she needed two witnesses from Poland who had known Simon and her. Fortunately, she was able to furnish witnesses. This birth certificate in the French language stamped by the judge is the only birth certificate Teddy would have.

Felicia had to work. In order to financially support herself and Teddy, she placed Teddy temporarily in an orphanage outside Paris, in Malmaison. That village is renowned for its having been one of the homes of the empress Josephine. Felicia believed the orphanage, with its lovely, spacious rooms and healthy children's routines, to be a good thing for her son.

Teddy cried when she left him at the home. The head teacher advised Felicia not to visit for a while and let her son become adjusted to the routine. Eventually, she saw him on Sunday afternoons. One day, when she arrived, there was a sad-faced boy in Teddy's room. When the boy left, Teddy announced, "Mother, don't bring me much or give me too many hugs. Pierre has neither a mother nor father. I don't want to make him unhappy."

Walking home from school, Teddy would occasionally go to a boulangerie and buy a baguette, one of his favorite foods. He would go back in a circuitous route so as to not need to share this treat.

The Hungarian couple who ran the home gave the children a sense of belonging, security, and warmth. Substantial, delicious meals were served, helping the children who had suffered poor nutrition during the war.

Teddy became a student in the village school. Teachers in the village school were greatly respected. One fellow student of Teddy's dared to talk back to a teacher, and the outraged elder man picked up the unfortunate lad by the heels, and a myriad of marbles of all shapes and sizes scattered to the floor.

Felicia found a job working for the Paris branch of a Polish news agency. Her language gifts proved invaluable. Being in a busy office and wearing a new business suit gave her a boost. She had some eccentric coworkers who had also experienced difficult times. One man rarely talked and disappeared for days at a time. When he did work, however, his journalism showed superior quality. After Felicia developed a rapport with the man, he disclosed to her that his mother kept him hidden in a closet for most of the war. That accounted for his erratic behavior.

Felicia's job proved to be difficult. Her boss constantly grabbed cigarettes from his workers. He also made unreasonable demands. One evening, he ordered Felicia to write a letter for him after office hours. She refused and began to walk out.

"You're fired," he yelled. He trailed after her like a lost puppy.

Felicia continued to walk out, and the boss later phoned her at home and apologized for his behavior. Felicia returned to work the next day as usual.

Felicia and Edward were married. Paris bloomed with spring flowers. A wonderful aroma of freshly baked bread wafted out boulangerie windows. Couples at sidewalk cafés daintily feasted on pastry together and slowly sipped *café*.

Felicia and Edward found a small apartment in a good neighborhood. The location was in École Militaire. It was a fifth floor walkup.

For Felicia, living in post-war Paris had a lot to offer, especially in the realm of the arts. Felicia said, "I need culture like concerts and the theatre as I need food and water!"

One day, a friend of her brother Stasiek arrived for a visit. The woman, wearing a Chanel suit, gloves, hat, and veil, was at first impressed by the upscale address. After climbing the five flights of stairs, she changed her mind.

Teddy was becoming well-adjusted to his current home and village school. The home had an arrangement to spend a month in the south of France for a summer vacation. The group took a train ride to Marseilles, and then the students would make up pairs or trios and have group hitchhiking for the rest of the journey. The school arranged for the group to stay at a large rented house. One day, in transit to the vacation house, Teddy and a few of his bedraggled friends from the home had slept on fire hoses on the rocky beach of Nice. The next day, unknowingly being in front of a police station, thumbs up and hitchhiking, the boys were picked up and jailed by Nice police. Ted and his friends appeared to be runaways. The boys, escorted to a nearby convent for soup, were also gently given bread by kindly nuns. Soon they were released from custody to a counselor from the home. They continued on the travels to the vacation house.

The Hungarian house mother and father who ran the orphanage occasionally lost their composure. The woman, a stunning brunette with a manner of goading her husband, made the usually gentle man at times explode in uncontrollable rage. Fortunately, these episodes were rare.

Occasionally, the woman would give an order that sounded unreasonable to a boy. The boy might disobey. While the boy was asked to go to the basement to retrieve an item, the door would be locked for one to two hours, and the boy would be unable to get back in for a time. That was the punishment.

Fond of baths and hot showers, especially since there had been such a dearth of refreshing cleansing during involuntary travels and years in camps, the boys took advantage of rations of the treats. The home had a policy of one to two showers a week, and after a certain length of time (usually about five minutes), a supervisor would pound on the door. The crafty boys learned that very early in the morning, there was hot water (a fresh supply) in the water tank, and Ted and friends would sneak down to the basement and indulge in the wonderful luxury of bathing. The house mother, although infuriated at the low supply of hot water, fortunately (for them) never caught the rascals.

Six years after she began work at the Polish government news agency, going to the office one morning, Felicia found a chaotic mass of varied persons at the agency's outside door.

At the fringe of the crowd, her eccentric journalist friend shouted out, "Leave, go home, and never come back here!"

Felicia obeyed this command.

Felicia, never aware of clandestine activities during her time at the agency, learned later that the agency had been shut down by the French authorities. The boss had been arrested by French gendarmes. It was rumored the boss had been accused of spying. He was deported to Poland.

Edward became reunited with his son Henri, a brilliant science student. Henri had been in college in Europe as war broke out. Having fled to England, he became part of the Poland-in-Exile Army. Henri married a stunning Finnish woman. The couple planned to immigrate to Canada and eventually go on to the United States.

News came that the home at Malmaison would be closing, and boys (like Teddy) must move to another place. Felicia arranged for Teddy to be returned to her care.

The French village school announced the year's end ceremony. Grades were read out with the lowest scores to the highest. Teddy always thought this rite of passage was cruel to those who had done poorly. He had done well at the school.

Felicia and Edward made the decision to immigrate to the United States with Teddy. Felicia's sister and brother-in-law, who were now in Chicago, agreed to sponsor them.

Seven years after arriving in Paris, Felicia, Teddy, and Edward would leave for the United States. The next great challenge would be that of another language change. Teddy spoke Polish and French fluently but no English. Edward spoke Polish, French, some Russian, and little English. Felicia, being an especially gifted linguist, spoke Polish, Russian, German, French, and English. A great opportunity in a new continent, a new life beckoned.

Teddy as Teenager

Felicia in Paris

CHAPTER 18

Europe to the United States 1950

It was fitting that Felicia, Teddy, and Edward's journey to the New World began in Genoa, Italy, the northern Italian birthplace of Columbus. Next to their hotel was a mausoleum with statues of famous natives of Genoa, including Columbus. Teddy, now fifteen years old, enjoyed his time there. He even left the hotel to see a movie. Intermissions had brief entertainment and included dancing girls. He handled well being in a strange city, taking the trams even though he didn't understand or speak Italian.

Despite the ship, ***The Argentine***, not being a luxury liner, the three "without a country" expressed happy anticipation to be on their way to the land of freedom and opportunity.

Atlantic Ocean storms caused the ship to pitch and roll. Moans and whining and other complaints could be heard from the passengers sprawled in passageways and on stairs. In spite of the turbulence, some brave Italian amateur musicians brought out accordions and played squeaky, off-key folk tunes. The impromptu concert with a background of moaning turned into a comic event.

This voyage reminded Felicia of a past travel when she and her first husband, Simon, traveled from Poland to Goteborg, Sweden. On the Baltic cruise, a storm developed during the voyage, and the rolling of the ship made it a challenge for passengers to remain upright. Finally, arriving at the dock, they found a taxi driver to take them around to view parks and get a feeling for the city and country. They stopped at a café for lunch. The next taxi driver spoke only Swedish. He didn't understand their Polish. The couple presented the driver with a card that had the name of a museum.

Suddenly, the driver took an acute turn to a small country road. A small cemetery was spied ahead. Were they to be robbed? Were they to be killed? The mysterious driver then stopped the cab by the side of the road, gently closing his door. He took off his cap and motioned for Simon to remove his hat. The driver stood at attention by a modest tombstone. It was finally realized that the driver's parents were buried there. He didn't often get this way to visit. After realizing this, they enjoyed the trip to the museum, and much later, back to the boat dock and to the sea voyage home to Poland.

Felicia's mind jolted back to current times as the Italian ship drew near to Gibraltar. Felicia hoped to explore the historic landmark. Unfortunately for her, stateless persons were not allowed to disembark.

In New York, an organization set up to aid immigrants assisted the trio in every way and helped them in their quest to go to Chicago, where Felicia's beloved sister, brother-in-law, and their two children lived. Felicia's sister would be her sponsor.

In Chicago, Felicia found a job at a lamp factory, where the considerate boss helped her when she asked him to talk to her as if to a child for a while. She could read English well but needed practice in speaking the language. Her dignified boss, in his Brooks Brothers suit, kept opening and closing desk drawers to explain to her what a desk looked like. The demonstration, although elementary to her, showed his concern. He wanted her to be successful.

Teddy spoke little English and soon enrolled in a good Chicago high school. The supportive French teacher helped him enormously. He audited (sat in) classes the first semester. He was a fine student. Teddy found a part-time job in a library connected to a church. He worked with two black students, and they all got along well. However, his English not being on a high level, having seen the word "slave" in a book and believing it meant someone who worked hard, said to his coworkers, "Let's get to work, slaves!" The two headed for him with clenched fists until they realized his language limits and forgave him for the mistake.

Felicia was so happy to be reunited with her sister and brother-in-law. She adored her niece and nephew—lovely and smart children. On weekends, her sister and brother-in-law would take them all in his car and show them the countryside around Chicago.

Still, Chicago was not such a good fit for Felicia. The family soon looked into a way to settle in New York; Edward went ahead to find a job and an apartment there.

CHAPTER 19

Manhattan
Early 1950s

Edward found an apartment for Felicia, Teddy, and himself. Edward's son was now in the vicinity. Edward adored his son, daughter-in-law, and grandchildren. He was anxious to spend more time with them. Felicia waited for Teddy to complete the year of high school in Chicago before the move halfway across the country.

The new apartment, located in the upper west side of Manhattan, provided a doorman for purposes of safety and assisting tenants. The neighborhood had good public transportation and convenient shopping; the sidewalks teemed with fruit and vegetable kiosks. The smell of freshly-baked bread drifted onto the sidewalk. Those were comforting reminders of the time in Paris. After World War II, the vitality of markets and culture were revitalized.

European émigrés like themselves were attracted to neighborhood life. Frequently, sounds of a pianist or violinist honing his or her craft streamed out from an open window. A multitude of languages could be heard from the street. Felicia's family answered the phone in Polish and spoke Polish at home. But the family was fortunate to be fluent in English and French as well. The family had spoken Russian, which was a reminder of a difficult time. Many described the Europe left behind as the "other side." Felicia tried to erase the sad memories of World War II; those recollections at times seemed too fresh.

Shortly after the move to New York City, Felicia began work as a statistical clerk at an adoption agency. Her skills in keeping statistics in the Russian work camp proved helpful after all. Felicia discovered through a mutual friend that her former cousin by marriage, Harry, whom she had last seen in prewar Warsaw, had survived the war and was living in Manhattan. She showed up in Harry's apartment entrance and rang the doorbell. She announced her visit on a speakerphone. At first, he refused to see her.

"Felicia, I thought you were dead!"

Finally, Felicia spied feet slowly descending the staircase leading from the apartment of Harry. Felicia waited anxiously, shifting the weight of her feet from one to the other.

With a stunned look, Harry gave her a long hug. Harry and Felicia both had tears streaming down their faces. They resumed a life-long friendship, only interrupted by the war years.

Edward worked as a cutter in the garment district of NYC. Edward also started a real estate company with a partner and liked this new challenge. Felicia became treasurer of the real estate company. The couple played bridge and renewed social contacts with old friends from Poland who were in similar circumstances to theirs. The friends all had fascinating real-life stories about the war years and how they lived and survived by good choices and amazing luck. There were miracles!

Teddy finished high school and college in NYC. He eventually graduated from medical school. Teddy, having gone through the chaotic life experience during World War II times, has lived without bitterness. This helped shape him into a benevolent and humane person. He believes in justice for all. He treats others fairly and expects others to treat him justly. He has a great sense of humor. This trait has helped him in life as it aided his mother, Felicia, through challenging times.

Felicia often expressed that of all her deeds, the achievement of which she was the most proud was that she saved her child.

That happened when she and Teddy were Stalin's guests.